experiencing

F R E E D O M

A Study in Galatians

Name _____

experiencing
F R E E D O M
A Study in Galatians

Five Day Format

Each lesson is divided into a five-day study plan. This is only a recommended way to divide your study. You may use this recommendation or another plan of your choosing.

Digging Deeper

Some of the lessons will contain a section labeled "Digging Deeper."
These optional sections provide the opportunity for additional study.

Memory Verse

Each lesson will have a memory verse.
The verse can be learned for the week the lesson is discussed in your group.

Contributors

Emily Dempster is a biblical counselor. She has a deep passion to see women defined not by their circumstances but by who they were created to be. She has earned her Masters of Arts in Pastoral Counseling from Liberty University Theological Seminary. Married 16 years to Ryan, they have two busy middle school children. Emily enjoys exercise, reading, watching soccer and traveling with her family.

Julie Bernard serves as the Women's Ministry Director at Salem Heights Church. She loves the team approach to ministry and encouraging and developing Women's Ministry leaders. She enjoys drinking coffee with friends, snuggling with her four grandchildren, and golfing with her husband.

Tara Cox currently serves as the Girls' Night Out Coordinator for Salem Heights Church Women's Ministry. She graduated from Corban University with a B.S. in Biblical Studies and is hoping to complete her Master's Degree. She spends most of her time chasing, dancing, reading to and otherwise growing up her three girls alongside her husband. She has a passion to see others come to know and love God through the study of His Word.

Angi Greene serves with college-age students in the Cross Road Ministry at Salem Heights Church. She is also involved in biblical counseling and enjoys ministering with her husband to couples preparing for marriage. She treasures opportunities to disciple and mentor women as she encourages them to love God and His Word. She loves spending time with her husband, daughter and two sons. Reading, running and baking are a few of her hobbies.

Joanne Mueller loves God's Word and enjoys encouraging others to study the Bible for themselves. She earned her Bachelor of Arts degree in English, and, on most days, it is difficult to find any surface space in her home because every inch is cluttered with the various books that she has started reading. Her days are filled with her husband and two children who love to hike and fish in the Oregon outdoors.

Gina Weigand has been married to her high school sweetheart for over 35 years and they have two grown children. She loves spending time with her family, gardening, and attending musical theatre.

experiencing
F R E E D O M
A Study in Galatians

Table of Contents

experiencing
FREEDOM
A Study in Galatians

Workbook Lessons

Lesson One

Scandalous Grace

The gospel is good news! The gospel is the good news of our salvation through Christ coming to earth, dying on the cross, rising on the third day, and ascending into heaven. By grace, through faith in Christ, we can have life with Jesus—eternal life, and we can live out that eternal life today in freedom. Then why do we live like we aren't free? Why do we live in bondage to other people's opinions? Why do we try to do everything just right in order to gain or keep God's favor? Paul writes this letter about gospel freedom to the Galatian church, a group of believers.

Paul did not begin his life as Paul but as Saul, a Jewish Pharisee. He was zealous for the Law of Moses, which was given by God to the Israelites. Because salvation through the New Testament Gospel is granted by grace instead of adherence to the Old Testament Law, Saul persecuted the early Christians. He even witnessed the stoning of the Christian martyr Stephen. Saul believed the gospel after encountering Jesus on the road to Damascus. Afterward, Saul was known as the Apostle Paul.

In writing to the Galatians, Paul aimed to disprove the teaching that we need to uphold the Jewish Law in addition to our faith in Christ in order to obtain salvation. Galatia was a province of the Roman Empire and was located in central Asia Minor. This letter, sometimes referred to as an epistle, was circulated amongst several Christian churches in Galatia. Paul wrote to them the good news that they were free, indeed. They did not have to keep the Law anymore. This good news is for us, as well. We can freely live out our eternal life today. What does this freedom look like?

Day 1

Read Galatians Chapters 1 and 2

1. What are you hoping to gain as you study Galatians this year?

2. From chapter 1, identify why this book was written.

Digging Deeper

Using a commentary or the introduction to Galatians in your Bible, record some facts about the book in general that would be helpful to keep in mind as you begin this study.

---

3. What thoughts come through your mind as you think about the purpose of this book?

Day 2

Read Galatians 3

4. List the questions Paul asks in 3:1-7. What point is Paul trying to make?

5. Paul introduces another person in this chapter. What facts did you learn about him?

6. Identify repeated words, phrases, or ideas from chapter 3. As you read through your list, what words are you excited to learn more about or what ideas are new to you? Write out any questions you may have.

Day 3

Read Galatians 4

7. What amazing news does Paul share in Galatians 4:1-7?

8. How does this same news encourage you today?

9. List some concerns Paul has for the church in Galatians 4. In what ways are these same concerns valid today?

Day 4

Read Galatians 5

10. Galatians 5:1 can be identified as a key verse for the book. Summarize this verse in your own words.

11. What repeated words, ideas, or phrases can you identify in this chapter? What questions do you have as you begin your study?

12. The Holy Spirit is identified in this chapter. What do you already know about the Holy Spirit? What can you learn from this chapter?

Day 5

Read Galatians 6

13. Put yourself in the Galatians' shoes. What impact would Paul's words in Galatians 6 have on you?

14. Why might Galatians close in this way? What are Paul's closing thoughts?

15. What is your overall reaction to the book of Galatians?

16. What do you think is the main message of the book?

17. In what ways is this book applicable to you right now? How about to the world we live in today?

Lesson Two
Knowing the One True Gospel

Memory Verse

"For I delivered to you as of first importance what I also received, that Christ died for our sins according to the Scriptures, and that He was buried, and that He was raised on the third day according to the Scriptures"
1 Corinthians 15:3-4

When we come to the book of Galatians, we are in essence entering into a spiritual battleground. One that has been waged since the very first time sin entered this world... One we will continue to face until Jesus returns. When sin first dawned in the human heart, God promised the remedy, a Savior that would one day come and make right all that went wrong. He would restore the relationship that was broken; we could once again walk with the Living God, fully forgiven and free. Until that time, God would give us a tutor to lead us to Christ; the Law He gave to Moses. This Law would govern His people, Israel, until it could be fulfilled through the sacrifice of the perfect Lamb of God. It would show us that no matter how hard we tried, it was impossible to live up to God's righteous standards on our own. We would always fail, and there would always be a sacrifice to pay. However, the cross of Jesus ushered in a new covenant, fulfilling the Law, and freeing us to live anew—the old covenant that God put into place through Moses was no longer required for salvation. The believers of Paul's day, however, were succumbing to the temptation to add to God's provision of salvation through the cross. That temptation is still with us today. Paul shows up to defend the freedom we have in the Gospel of Christ.

Day 1

1. When did you first hear the gospel? What did you think?

2. How does Paul introduce himself in verse 1?

3. Read Luke 6:13 and Acts 1:21-26. What were the qualifications of an apostle?

4. Read Acts 9:1-15 and 1 Corinthians 15:3-10. How was Paul qualified to be an apostle?

5. When you consider *who* the author is, what significance does this have for the rest of the book?

Day 2

6. We can gain better insight into a book when we compare it with others. In this next section, compare the greeting in Galatians with Paul's greeting in other books. Use the chart to record **observations of tone** in the introductions and **specific words used to greet** the readers.

Passage	Observations
Ephesians 1:1-6	
Philippians 1:2-8	
Colossians 1:2-4	
Galatians 1:1-6	

Key Term

Apostle: One sent on a mission. The term originally referred to the twelve disciples chosen by Christ during His earthly ministry. These were the men who were closest to the Christ, were taught by Him personally, and witnessed the miracles that proclaimed His deity, along with His crucifixion and resurrection. Jesus empowered them to perform miracles such as healing and casting out demons — these proved their divine authority as representatives and spokesmen of God. In the early stages of the church, these men were essential in setting up the foundations of the church and were used to grow the church by spreading the good news of the Gospel of Christ.

7. What insights do these introductions give you into the importance of Paul's message to the Galatians?

8. If you were the one who received this letter, what would you be thinking?

9. How is Paul's love for God and His people evident in how he is addressing them?

Day 3

Reread Galatians 1:1-10

10. What are Paul's issues with the churches in Galatia in verses 6-10?

11. Use 1 Corinthians 15:1-4 to define the term "gospel."

Digging Deeper

Scan the book of Acts looking at the passages where Paul is preaching the gospel. Find at least two to three accounts and write down how he uses the key elements of the gospel (as defined in question 12) in each occasion. Record your thoughts and observations below.

12. In Galatians 1:6, Paul refers to "a different gospel." Read 2 Corinthians 11:3-4. What insights do you gain about this phrase?

13. In what ways is the gospel being distorted today?

14. What are some ways you can be sure that you don't fall into the same trap as the Galatians when it comes to living free in the gospel?

Day 4

Review Galatians 1:1-10

15. What strong language does Paul use in verses 8-9?

16. Look up the word "accursed" in the dictionary and record the definition here.

17. To whom are these accusations directed?

18. Why do you think God would lead Paul to use this term when it comes to someone teaching a different gospel?

19. How do Paul's warning in verses 8-9 apply to your life today?

Read Galatians 1:6-10

20. Summarize in your own words what Paul is saying in verse 10.

21. How is Paul's passion for the purity of the gospel evident to these statements?

22. What is he implying about those who are teaching a different gospel?

23. Look back to Galatians 1:3-4. What is the truth that Paul shares in these verses? How does that impact your heart?

24. Pray for discernment throughout the week. Ask God to show you when a different gospel is being presented. (Consider what you read, what you see, and what you hear.) How does believing the true gospel give you hope and freedom?

Lesson Three

Who is Paul?

Memory Verse

"For I would have you know, brethren, that the gospel which was preached by me is not according to man."
Galatians 1:11

In this lesson, there are a few important terms that will be helpful to understand. The word *Judaism* refers to the religious system that had once been established by God through the Law given to Abraham but had since morphed into a man made religious system that depended on a person's ability to keep these laws in order to appear righteous before men and God. It was a system of works. One of the most important "works" that concerned the Jewish community of that day was the work of circumcision. Since the Church was now made up of both Jews (who would be circumcised under the Law) and Gentiles (who would be considered "uncircumcised") this was a dividing issue. These terms and concepts may or may not be new to you. Though they don't seem to have anything to do with our life today, there are important spiritual implications that relate directly to your life and mine.

Day 1

1. Often times a chosen career requires passing certain requirements. How have you, or someone you know, met the required standards of a particular career?

Read Galatians 1:11-24

2. In what ways does Paul describe the gospel he preached (verses 11-12)?

3. What are some phrases Paul used to describe who he was before he encountered Christ (verses 13-14)?

4. What were the steps in the process of Paul's calling (verses 15-16a)? Choose at lease one term or phrase that stands out to you to look up and summarize it here.

Day 2

Read Acts 9:1-24

5. What in Paul's story is amazing to you?

6. Where do you see evidence of a changed life?

7. How does reading this passage in Acts help you better understand the Galatians passage?

Digging Deeper

Learn More About Paul
What else can we learn about Paul from the following passages?

2 Corinthians 11:21-33

Acts 20:17-38

Acts 26:2-23

Reread Galatians 1:16-24

8. Complete the chart below noting what Paul did and did not do after his conversion.

DID DO	DID NOT DO

9. According to the insights from the chart above, what do Paul's actions reveal about the source of the gospel he received?

10. Why would this be important to the churches in Galatia?

Day 4

Reread Galatians 1:16-24

11. How did the conversion of Paul impact the Church? What was the ultimate result (verses 23-24)?

12. Overall, why does Paul's story matter in the context of this letter? Why should it matter to you?

13. Recall a time when you heard the powerful testimony of someone who came to believe in Christ. How did it impact you?

14. Reread Galatians 1:15-16a with yourself in mind. How do you respond to the fact that God chose YOU personally in these ways just as He chose Paul? Write a short prayer in response.

15. Take time to write out your story. Where has God called you from and where are you now? Remember all of our stories, whether we think they are significant or not, are important to God. After all He writes our stories. You may want to write it on a separate paper or in the side bar "notes" section.

Day 5

Read Psalm 78

This psalm is about God's persistent redemption of His people.

16. Identify in this psalm the characteristics of people that forget to be thankful for God's grace in their lives.

17. After reading this psalm, reflect on the importance of sharing your story with others and the next generation.

18. What happens if we don't?

19. What are the benefits if we do?

Notes

Lesson Four

What Exactly do we Need to do?

Memory Verse

"For indeed circumcision is of value if you practice the Law; but if you are a transgressor of the Law, your circumcision has become uncircumcision."
Romans 2:25

At the very beginning of the Church, there was a debate among Jewish Christians regarding the keeping of the Law of Moses. Paul had been on his first missionary journey, and God was miraculously saving Gentiles! The Church was growing, and many were rejoicing as they saw the work of God extending beyond the nation of Israel. Because of what God was doing in growing His Church, Paul was sent back to Jerusalem to the center of the Church in that day to meet with the leaders and come up with a consensus. Was it necessary for Gentile Christians to follow the Jewish Law in order to be saved?

Day 1

Read Galatians 2:1-10

1. What details does Paul give about his trip to Jerusalem in Galatians 2:1-2?

2. What were some problems Paul encountered when he went to Jerusalem (verses 3-4)?

3. What was Paul's main concern in his defense (verse 5)? How should we apply his same concern?

4. Compare Paul's calling to that of Peter (verses 7-8).

5. What were the results of meeting with the "pillars" of the church (verses 9-10)?

Day 2

| Read Acts 15:1-11 |

Acts 15 records how the Church went about resolving this conflict at Jerusalem in the early days following Paul's first missionary journeys. This is known in Church history as The Jerusalem Council. The details in Acts add dimension to the events that took place in Galatians 2.

6. What were some men teaching in verses 1 and 5?

7. Peter was elected to be the messenger of the gospel to the Jews. What did he stand up and say in Jerusalem to defend the gospel (verses 6-11)?

8. How does the account in Acts add to your understanding of what Paul is writing in Galatians 2:1-10?

Digging Deeper

Who is Barnabas?

Paul made several trips to Jerusalem with his friend and colleague, Barnabas. Read Acts 4:36 and Acts 11:24. Record additional information you learn about Barnabas. Is there someone in your life that is like a Barnabas to you? Which of Barnabas' qualities would you like to emulate?

Day 3

Read Genesis 17:1-14

9. The Jewish people were often referred to as "the circumcised," while the Gentiles were among "the uncircumcised." What was the symbolism and significance of Jews being circumcised?

10. What reasons could you give for the importance Jews placed on circumcision?

11. Look up Deuteronomy 10:16; 30:6 and Jeremiah 9:25-26. What can you add to your understanding of circumcision from God's perspective? What were the Judaizers missing?

12. How are we, as believers, "circumcised"?

"And the LORD your God will circumcise your heart and the heart of your offspring, so that you will love the LORD your God with all your heart and with all your soul, that you may live."
Deuteronomy 30:6

Notice it is God who circumcises our hearts. Afterward, we are able to obey. His work precedes ours which is in response to what only He can do.

Day 4

> **Read Romans 2:25-29 and 4:9-16**

The Apostle Paul took up the issue of circumcision again in the book of Romans where Paul addresses believers in the Gentile city of Rome. Almost a decade after he first wrote to the Galatians, this issue was still a stumbling block for the Church.

13. What can we learn regarding circumcision that further validates the truth he is stating in our Galatians passage?

14. Read Philippians 3:4-7. How does Paul view his own circumcision?

15. Summarize what you have learned about circumcision and how the issue applies to you personally today. (Consider the list on the right.) How does what you have learned give you hope in your salvation?

Day 5

> **Reread Galatians 2:1-10**

It is important to remember that Paul was using this strong language with people he had previously taught. These were men and women who had had the benefit of his teaching for an extended period of time. Imagine being personally discipled by the Apostle Paul! This is why Paul was astonished that they had been deceived!

I think God should love and accept me because...

- ☑ I have obeyed enough.
- ☑ I am the perfect homemaker.
- ☑ I make homemade meals every night.
- ☑ I don't pursue any activities that do not involve my children or husband.
- ☑ I don't disagree with people — especially my husband.
- ☑ I only home school my children.
- ☑ I vote a certain way.
- ☑ I boycott places that support gay rights.
- ☑ When my children misbehave, I can quote verses to them.
- ☑ I only read Christian books and listen only to Christian music.
- ☑ I don't say no when someone makes a request of me.
- ☑ I am at church every time the doors are open.

We, however, will rub shoulders with many people around us who simply do not know the truth. They have never heard of the God who loves them, who sent His Son to die for them, and who desires to have a personal relationship with them. Even those who have heard, most have misconceptions about the gospel, Jesus Christ, and what is really means to know our Creator. We need to be careful with how we defend the truth with those who have never heard and treat them as Jesus would — with care, compassion and love.

16. How does your passion for the purity of the gospel show up when your beliefs do not line up with the beliefs of others?

17. How do we graciously defend the true gospel without demeaning others?

18. What is one way you can use Paul's example to stand up for the truth of the gospel in your own life right now?

19. What does it mean to serve God? Is it always in a church setting?

20. Where has God called you to serve Him? How can you use your gifts, training, and abilities this week for the Lord?

Notes

Lesson Five

What are They Gonna Think?

Memory Verse

"I have been crucified with Christ; and it is no longer I who live, but Christ lives in me; and the life which I now live in the flesh I live by faith in the Son of God, who loved me and gave Himself up for me."
Galatians 2:20

Imagine what it would be like to have lived devoutly one way, all your life, and then all of a sudden, things changed. Nothing was the same. This is what happened to the Jewish people. Before Christ, the Old Testament Law forbade the eating of certain foods. They also couldn't eat with certain people and had to eat in certain ways. Then Christ came and changed everything. This paradigm shift brought a whole new way of living and relating to God. Salvation or forgiveness no longer depended on your ability to live righteously by keeping the Law. Salvation was now fully accomplished on your behalf, through the death, burial, and resurrection of Christ. It was no longer about attaining righteousness through your own efforts – it was now all about Christ's righteousness *in* you.

Day 1

1. Describe a time in your life when you became fully convinced of something that you had previously believed to be wrong or untrue.

Read Galatians 2:11-21

In this section, the Apostle Paul opposes the Apostle Peter in Antioch "because he stood condemned." The NIV says "because he was wrong" (Galatians 2:11).

Read Acts 11:1-18

Let's discover the background for why Paul was using this kind of language with Peter.

2. What accusations were brought against Peter by those in Jerusalem (verses 2-3)?

3. What did Peter see in the vision that enabled him to respond to the accusations (verses 4-10)? Make a list.

4. In light of this experience, how do you account for Peter's actions when Paul encountered him in Galatians 2 (verses 12-14)?

5. Describe a time when you could relate with Peter (changing what you believe but then going back to your old behavior or activity). What caused you to get back on track to living free in the gospel?

Day 2

Read Galatians 2:11-21

To further illustrate his point regarding salvation, that it is by grace rather than a religious system of works, Paul recounts an incident that occurred in Antioch, Paul's home base during many years of his missionary journeys. Peter participated freely in meals where Jews and Gentiles ate together. However, there were still certain sects within the Jewish Christian community who believed that you had to abide by certain dietary and ceremonial laws. Instead of holding firm to what God had clearly taught him on this issue, when these Jews visited, Peter was drawn back into a system of works and did not sit with Gentiles. He tried to earn God's approval and favor through his actions instead of through his faith in Christ's payment on the cross.

6. What is going on in the heart (emotions) of Peter, and what actions show that he had strayed from living free in the gospel (verses 12-13)?

HEART	ACTIONS

7. What event or who caused Peter to change his behavior and how did his behavior affect those around him? Why is this significant?

8. What does it mean to "act hypocritically"? Look up the term in the dictionary and rewrite it in your own words.

9. Peter was struggling. He had fallen back into seeking to please people and to appear righteous before men (Galatians 1:10). His fear led to the actions described. Are there any areas of your life where you can see this pattern? (Areas to consider: your thoughts, activities, speech...)

Day 3

Reread Galatians 2:11-21

10. How did Paul confront Peter in verses 11 and 14?

11. Why is that significant? (Read 1 Timothy 5:19-21.)

12. What did Paul "see" as he looked at the situation? What point was Paul making in his statement in verse 14?

13. Why was it critical to the faith that Paul confront Peter on this issue? How does reading about this confrontation make you feel?

14. Most of the time, we are not going to find ourselves in the exact same position as Paul. How do we take the principle represented here and use it to gently remind other believers of our freedom — even when it comes to pleasing others or appearing one way and living another?

Day 4

Reread Galatians 2:11-21

15. What repeated term/phrase do you see in verses 16-17?

16. Look up the term "justified" in the dictionary and write the definition in your own words.

17. Fill in the chart below using verses 16-17 as your reference.

WE ARE MADE RIGHTEOUS VS. WE ARE NOT MADE RIGHTEOUS

Even though Peter knew better, his actions were communicating that our salvation and our sanctification (becoming more like Christ) was still based on some outer display of righteousness. In this case, he was acting like the religious Jews who depended on keeping the law in order to be saved. Peter had forgotten that Christ declared him fully justified – not on the basis of *his* works, but fully on the basis of Christ and His work on the cross.

18. How does knowing that Christ has declared YOU righteous, not by any work that you can do, but ONLY on the work He already completed on your behalf, keep you from going back to an old system of religious works to please God or look righteous to others?

Day 5

Reread Galatians 2:11-21

Just like Peter, we can fall into the trap of attempting to gain acceptance from God and others by our own efforts. Paul says three times in this passage that Jesus Christ, and not the Law, justifies us. God saves us by grace; we do not need to do anything to gain His acceptance!

19. Read Titus 3:3-7 and Ephesians 2:1-10. What do these verses indicate about God's acceptance of you? Note especially what it says about what *we* are able to do, and what *He* is able to do in our salvation.

20. How does a better understanding of grace in the gospel contribute to your appreciation of Paul's heart in Galatians 2:11-21?

21. Contrast the truth of the gospel with the teaching of the "men from James" or "circumcision party," otherwise known as Judaizers (verses 16-17). What can you learn from this contrast?

22. In verses 17-21, what statements does Paul make about a changed life to illustrate the importance of living free in the gospel of grace?

23. Read Galatians 2:20 and fill in the chart below noting what it says about YOU and what it says about GOD.

"I" STATEMENTS	"GOD" STATEMENTS

24. Now, read the above verse again with yourself in mind. How would your life change if you lived this out each day? What is one thing you can do this week to move yourself in this direction?

Lesson Six
Sidetracked—Part 1

Memory Verse

"For I am confident of this very thing, that He who began a good work in you will perfect it until the day of Christ Jesus."
Philippians 1:6

Paul begins his next argument by asking the Galatians if they had received the Holy Spirit through obeying the Law or through faith. We become more like Christ through the work of the Holy Spirit. If we are trying to bear spiritual fruit through obedience to the Law, we are striving in vain. We began with Christ through experiencing salvation by faith, and we received the Holy Spirit; we continue to grow in Christ through that same faith.

Day 1

1. Recall a time when you were headed for a destination and got off course. What happened?

Read Galatians 3:1-5

2. What unique terms does Paul use to describe the Galatians in verse 1? Look those up in a dictionary and record the definitions.

3. What do these terms tell you about the seriousness of Paul's message?

4. Paul asks a series of questions in verses 2-5. Rewrite the questions in your own words.

5. What had God done in the lives of the Galatians from verses 2-5? Make a list.

6. Look at the list above. God has done these for YOU if you have accepted Christ as your Savior! Thank Him for doing these things on your behalf.

Day 2

Reread Galatians 3:1-5

Let's look back at the terms we defined yesterday from verse 1. Two things had happened to the Galatians. First, they had allowed themselves to be charmed by something other than the truth of the gospel. Second, they were taught that the salvation they had received by faith in Christ was somehow incomplete. They believed that they needed to have Jesus plus something else... In this case, it was obedience to the Law. Because of this, they had become foolish, or dull of understanding. In essence, they were acting as if they had not been saved. They were not living free in the gospel!

7. Paul reminds them of something at the end of verse 1. What does he say?

8. How does the idea of being an eyewitness to an event solidify its truth in your heart?

Read 1 John 1:1-4

9. What phrases does John use to give credibility to what he is writing? List them below.

10. How does John's description of being an eyewitness to Christ bear testimony on the truth of what he is writing?

11. Recall how you first responded to the truth of Christ. How does remembering how you were first convinced keep you from falling away from living free in the gospel?

Day 3

Reread Galatians 3:1-5

The term "Spirit" is first introduced here in the book of Galatians and is used three times in five verses.

12. In your own words, what does Paul ask the Galatians in verse 2 (recall your answer from question 4)?

13. What are the two possible answers?

14. Look up each passage below and identify what each says about the Holy Spirit.

Romans 8:9

Ephesians 1:13

15. Given what you learned on the previous page, answer these questions:

    A. How did *you* receive the Spirit (verse 2, see also Romans 10:17)?

    B. What was *your* part? In other words, what can you take credit for (see also Ephesians 2:8-9)?

Day 4

We have seen from Scripture that we cannot do anything to receive the Holy Spirit in our lives. He is intimately involved in our salvation, He indwells us from that point on, and God did all of this when we believed. So, with that in mind, let's look at the next question Paul asks of the Galatians.

Reread Galatians 3:1-5

16. In verse 3, Paul uses two terms with the Spirit and the flesh. What are they?

17. Cross reference Philippians 1:6 and Hebrews 12:2a and record the similar terms that are used here. How would you use these truths to answer Paul's question to the Galatians in verse 3?

18. How do these terms relate to our salvation (accomplished when we believed) and our sanctification (the ongoing work of the Spirit as we grow in the Christian life)?

Digging Deeper

Look up "sanctification" (sanctify, sanctified, etc.) in a Bible Dictionary (there is usually one in the back of your Bible) and record your observations below.

19. The manner in which we receive the Spirit (salvation) and the way we grow in the Spirit (sanctification) differ according to Paul. When we review our own sanctification or growth differently than the Bible teaches, how do we get off track? How does a wrong view of the gospel in our everyday living cause us to want to add something of our own to our spiritual life?

Day 5

Reread Galatians 3:1-5

Paul sums up his questions by reminding them to not forget all that God had done in their lives through two other experiences.

20. What are the two final areas that Paul uses to support God's work among them? Write his questions again in your own words (verses 4-5).

21. In what ways do followers of Christ suffer?

22. Read John 16:33; Romans 5:3-5; Romans 8:18; 1 Peter 4:12-19; 5:10; and James 1:2-4. What part does suffering play in the life of a believer? What is God's purpose in our suffering? Pay special attention to the promises God gives us in suffering.

23. How have you seen God at work in your suffering?

24. What promises do you need to claim in your current situation, or as you anticipate trials that will come your way?

God is still a God of miracles. We see Him at work every time someone believes in Christ as they move from spiritual death to new life in Him, from spiritual blindness to seeing. We see it when we watch a believer walk through horrific suffering with hope, peace, and joy. When we experience God at work in our life in these ways, we cannot walk away from living in light of the gospel to a system of works.

25. Respond in thanksgiving to God for His saving you through no effort of your own, and for His work in you to conform you to the image of Christ. Thank Him for the miracles He has done and is doing in your life as you live victorious over sin. Praise Him for being the only One who can accomplish these things on your behalf.

Lesson Seven
Sidetracked—Part 2

Memory Verse

"Christ redeemed us from the curse of the Law, having become a curse for us — for it is written, 'CURSED IS EVERYONE WHO HANGS ON A TREE'"
Galatians 3:13

Paul uses Abraham as an illustration from Scripture for his argument that faith is credited to us as righteousness. Abraham, the father of the nation Israel, was a key figure for the Jews, but he also lived about four centuries *before* the Law was given to Moses. Therefore, he was the perfect example of what it means to be righteous in God's eyes apart from strict adherence to the Law. Abraham wasn't righteous because he was perfect. Although he had impressive accomplishments, he and his wife Sarah were raised in an idolatrous society. When God spoke to Abraham, he believed Him, and it was this faith that was reckoned to him as righteousness.

Day 1

Read Galatians 3:6-14

1. Think of someone you know that has achieved great things. What is it about the person you admire?

Read Genesis 12

2. What promises did God give to Abram (Abraham's name before God changed it)?

3. Where do you see Abram struggling to trust God in this passage?

Read Genesis 15:1-6

4. What did the Lord promise? What was Abram's response?

5. What does Galatians 3:6 say about Abraham?

6. Read Romans 4:1-5. Contrast what saved Abraham with what did not.

Day 2

Read Galatians 3:6-14

7. What other observations can you make from this passage regarding salvation?

8. How does Galatians 3:6-9 shed further light on the way both Jews and Gentiles are saved?

9. Think about the characteristics of God that are evident from the truths learned above. Write a prayer of thanksgiving in response to what these truths mean to you.

Day 3

Read Galatians 3:6-14

Continuing Paul's argument from Scripture, Paul uses a series of quotes from the Old Testament. These are marked in some Bibles with SMALL CAPITAL letters. In others, it is indicated by a reference next to or below the passage. Let's look at the first five quotes Paul used and discover what truth he is teaching through them.

10. List the five references in the chart below. With each reference, Paul makes a comment. Record Paul's comment and the quote from the Old Testament.

PAUL'S COMMENT	QUOTE FROM THE OLD TESTAMENT
1.	
2.	
3.	
4.	
5.	

11. For each of Paul's five comments, write the meaning in your own words.

12. What do these verses say about our ability to keep the Law?

13. Why do you think we try to please God through our own efforts?

14. What truths can you tell yourself today to help you from living this way?

Day 4

| Read Galatians 3:13-14 |

15. Paul's final quote from the Old Testament is recorded in verse 13. What does it say?

16. Paul makes a connection between the "Law" and "hanging on a tree." They are both "cursed." Why are they connected?

17. What did Christ do on our behalf, and what was the result (verse 13; Galatians 4:5)?

18. According to verse 14, what were the reasons Christ redeemed us?

19. Look at the Key Term at the side bar. How does this definition enlighten your understanding of all that Christ has done for you, especially considering what you learned today regarding the exchange Christ made for you? How does it encourage you to walk in the light of the gospel?

Day 5

> **Reread Galatians 3:6-14**

As you think back to the truths you learned in the past few days, reflect on the following questions. We can often be very blind to the ways we are still trying to earn God's favor instead of walking in the freedom that the gospel provides.

20. Do you ever find yourself relying on self-made "laws" to gain God's approval?

21. Do you sometimes give yourself a pass or fail in your Christian walk based on rules? Explain.

22. What things make you feel *more* accepted by God when you do them?

23. What makes you feel *less* accepted by God if you do not do them?

Redeemed: To buy out or from, as of purchasing a slave to set them free.

Some Areas We Try to Gain God's Acceptance or Approval:

☑ Spending time in God's Word (and how often)

☑ Scripture memorization

☑ Church attendance (and how often)

☑ Prayer (and how often)

☑ Being the perfect wife, mom, friend, servant, worker, student, etc.

☑ Staying away from certain "sins" or "gray areas"

24. Read Psalm 1. Why do we read God's Word, pray, etc.?

25. Write a prayer asking God to help you trust Christ alone for your salvation and for your ongoing relationship with Him.

Lesson Eight

Why the Law?

Memory Verse

"But the Scripture has shut up everyone under sin, so that the promise by faith in Jesus Christ might be given to those who believe."
Galatians 3:22

Paul finishes proving to his readers from evidence of the Old Testament that God's plan of salvation had always been about faith and not about works of the Law. Paul addresses the issue that he is sure his readers will ask: If the Law was not important for salvation, then why did God give the Law?

Day 1

1. Is there a law that you believe to be out of date or worthless?

> **Read Galatians 3:16-18**

When properly created, a contract is a legal binding document that both parties sign. If a change is made to the contract, both parties must agree. In verse 15, Paul compares the covenant in the Old Testament that was given to Abraham with a contract. The point is that a third party cannot come along and change a contract between the two original people.

2. Who made the promise, and to whom was it made (verse 16)?

3. Which two similar words are compared in verse 16?

4. What is the significance of those words? If this was a contract, who is it between? Who then has the authority to change the contract?

Digging Deeper

Galatians 3:16 refers to the offspring or seed. The conflict begins in Genesis 3:15 as Satan wanted to prevent the Seed, who would one day crush his head, from coming. Read through a few more passages in the New Testament. How do these passages help with your understanding of the term "Seed."

Romans 9:8

1 John 3:9

Romans 16:20

Day 2

430 years pass between the confirmation of this promise and when Moses received the Law at Sinai, but Paul's point is clear: the Law given cannot change the covenant given earlier to Abraham. It continued to be in effect. What exactly is the Law then?

5. Read the definition in the side bar. How does this help you understand the Law Paul is referring to?

6. Skim Exodus 20-24 paying attention to the chapter headings and subheadings in your Bible. What can you learn about the Law from these chapters?

7. What is the reasoning in Exodus 20:20 for the Law being given?

8. How do you think the Law will accomplish this? Can we ever keep the whole Law perfectly?

9. If we can't keep the whole Law perfectly, what really do we need?

Day 3

Read Galatians 3:19-20

10. Paul poses a question in verse 19. What answers can you find in verses 19-20 to his question?

11. What time restraints were placed on the Law? How was that different than the promise with Abraham?

12. Read Romans 8:1-4. In what ways has the Law, which was given temporarily, been fulfilled?

13. What hope does this give someone trying to "keep the Law" to earn God's love and approval?

Day 4

Read Galatians 3:21-26

14. Paul asks another question in verse 3:21. What answers can you find from:

Verse 3:21 _____
What could it give?

Verses 3:19a, 22 _____
What is the significance of this?

Verses 3:23-26 _____

Look at the definition to the right. Paul compares the Law to a "tutor." What was the purpose of the tutor in verse 24? Without a "tutor" what do our lives look like?

The Law and the promise work together to show sinners their inability to keep the Law and, thus, they reveal our need for Jesus as Savior.

15. What freedom does this passage provide you from becoming exhausted from trying to keep a bunch of rules to earn God's love and approval?

Day 5

Because we are not bound by a list of rules, we must pursue a life of grace. Thank God for His grace on your life and for saving you with no ability to keep the Law. Because of this salvation, you are new in Christ.

16. Read Ephesians 2:1-9. Use the chart to contrast who we were before Christ with who we are after Christ (verses 1-6).

BEFORE CHRIST	AFTER CHRIST

17. List what is involved in our salvation according to verses 7-9?

Key Term

Tutor: The Greek word denotes a slave who had the duty of taking care of a child until adulthood. The "tutor" would escort the children to and from school and watch over their behavior at home. Tutors were often strict disciplinarians, causing those under their care to yearn for the day when they would be free from the tutor's custody. (*Galatians: The Wondrous Grace of God*, MacArthur, p. 55)

18. How would you use Ephesians 2:1-9 with someone who believes that keeping a list of rules to earn God's love and acceptance would lead a person to heaven?

19. What is one truth from this study that is impacting you the most? Share that with a friend or family member today.

Lesson Nine

Living as an Adopted Child

Memory Verse

"But when the fullness of the time came, God sent forth His Son, born of a woman, born under the Law, so that He might redeem those who were under the Law, that we might receive the adoption as sons."
Galatians 4:4-5

The Galatian believers had been enslaved to false religions. God saved them and set them free, but now they were returning to enslavement, this time to the Law. They traded one form of bondage for another. Paul says that the things to which they were enslaving themselves are "weak and worthless" because they cannot justify the Galatians or energize them for godly living.

The Law is stifling. It makes every decision and determines every step. Maturity and freedom are not the goal of the Law. The Law simply mandates every move and every decision. The Law focuses on outward appearance and does nothing to encourage and stimulate growth. Paul uses the metaphor of a legal guardian to help us understand the limitations of the Law. It is important to understand that in Rome a child was under the care and control of a legal guardian. The child was not much different than a slave. In fact, he might as well have been one. The Galatians were living just like children under the care and control of their legal guardian.

Day 1

1. What freedoms would you give a teenager living in your home that you would not give a toddler?

Read Galatians 4:1-7

2. What similarities are there between a child and a slave? What are the differences in regards to dependence?

3. In the same way that a child in Rome was under the care of a legal guardian, the believers were living as if they were under obligation to the Law, enslaved to the "elementary principles of the world." In other words, they were living under the weight of legalism. What areas of life are believers susceptible to living controlled by rules and regulations today?

Digging Deeper

Using a commentary or your study Bible notes to learn more about cultural issues regarding coming of age and to gain more insight into the function of guardians and stewards (or managers) mentioned in Galatians 4:2.

---

4. How does living this way mirror living as a child being managed by a guardian?

5. Prayerfully consider your own life. Is it possible that there are areas that you are living as one enslaved to rules and regulations? (See sidebar for ways women try to gain the approval and favor of God.) If so, what might they be? How would living this way keep you from maturing?

I think God should love and accept me because...

☑ I always read my Bible in the morning.

☑ I'm a good friend.

☑ I follow the law, like not stealing and following the speed limit.

☑ I go to church every Sunday.

☑ I take care of my house and yard.

☑ I'm not in debt.

☑ I've been faithful to my husband.

☑ I don't say no when someone makes a request of me.

Day 2

Read Galatians 4:1-7

6. What were God's reasons for sending His son?

7. Look up "redemption" in a dictionary. Describe redemption in your own words.

God has been in the business of redemption from the beginning. The entire Bible is a story of God's grace and the redemption of His people. When Adam and Eve sinned in the garden and broke their relationship with God, the result was death and woe. Yet God loved His people so much He provided a way to restore the relationship. The Good News is that He sent His Son. We, however, still live in a broken world, and in this world, God is reaching down into the brokenness and is redeeming lives.

8. Record what you learn about redemption through the following verses.

   Galatians 3:13

   Colossians 1:13-14

   Titus 2:11-14

God not only wants to redeem us from eternal death, but he wants to redeem us from a life that is not experiencing freedom. He wants us to have our life from Him, not from the things around us such as comparing ourselves to others, the expectations we have placed on ourselves and others, and the sufferings of life.

9. What does Romans 8:18-25 say about our present sufferings and the redemption Christ provides?

10. What hope does this verse provide?

The good news for a child living under the control of a guardian comes the day his father decides it is time for him to be recognized as an adult with all the rights and responsibilities of an heir (verse 2). No longer is he obligated to live as a slave. Good news has come to us as well! God sent His Son (verse 5) and we are redeemed people that can live free!

11. Write a brief statement about redemption; include where it comes from, what its purpose is and the results in your life.

12. In what ways does understanding that Jesus provided this redemption for you encourage you to no longer live under the weight of trying to earn God's love and acceptance?

Day 3

Read Galatians 4:1-7

Not only did God send His Son to redeem us, but He provided for us to be adopted into His family as well! The Law could never have made us daughters of God, but he chose us.

13. Can you think of a special adoption story either from someone you know or yourself? What makes the story special?

14. How does this picture help you to understand the picture of adoption from this verse?

15. Read Romans 8:12-17. What does a child look like that has received the spirit of adoption as a son?

16. How does this encourage you to live differently in your present circumstances?

Day 4

Read John 14:15-20, 25-26

As part of God's redemption and adoption as His daughters, we were sent the Spirit of His Son into our hearts. God has gone to great lengths to comfort His people. First, He sent His Son, and then He gave us His Spirit. He gave us Jesus to rescue us from eternal death but also provided His Spirit to guide us to live in this broken world. He cares about our everyday attitudes and actions and gives us His Spirit to help.

17. What truths does Christ tell His disciples about the Spirit?

18. How do these qualities of the Holy Spirit apply to the struggle of living free in a broken world?

19. Where do you currently need to rely on the Holy Spirit in your everyday life?

It is significant that Paul says "Because you are sons, God has sent forth the Spirit of His Son into our hearts, crying 'Abba! Father!'" (Galatians 4:6) Household slaves were forbidden to address the head of the family as "Abba." This was a privilege reserved only for the true child.

20. Daddy, an endearing title! The title Jesus, the Son of God, used when referring to God the Father. Read Mark 14:32-36. What does Jesus' prayer reveal about His relationship with God the Father?

21. When you think of the privilege we have to call God, "Daddy," how does that make you feel?

22. Read Romans 8:1-17. List the benefits that are yours because God is your Father.

23. Considering what Jesus' prayer revealed about His relationship with God the Father and the benefits that are yours because God is also your Father, evaluate if you are living as a slave to the Law or an heir of the living God. Thank God for being your "Abba Father."

Review Galatians 4:1-7 and Romans 8:1-25

24. Reflect on the truths that you are redeemed and adopted. Thank the Lord for providing His Son to save you and His Spirit to guide you as you live in this broken world.

Abba, Father (7:3): Signifying one that provides, protects and supports.

Lesson Ten

Biblical Convictions Versus Personal Preferences

Memory Verse

"Whether, then, you eat or drink or whatever you do, do all to the glory of God."
1 Corinthians 10:31

When a child learns to read, it opens up a whole new world. He can understand and learn about so many new things. Even reading street and store signs expands his world. After a child learns to read, we expect him to read. We would think something was wrong if he just sat contently reading his alphabet time and time again.

We can compare this analogy to the Galatian believers. Before they believed the gospel, the Galatian believers were enslaved to false religions. They worshiped fertility gods tied to the sun and moon. God saved them and set them free. However, they returned to enslavement. This time, it was to the Law of the Old Testament. They traded one form of bondage in false religion for another and remained in a life lived without freedom. They continued seeking to earn God's acceptance and love.

Day 1

Read Galatians 4:8-11

1. Give examples of skills you learn that you never forget.

2. What word does Paul use in verse 8 that describes the status of Galatian believers? Compare and contrast the word with freedom.

3. Instead of false religion and idols, what were the Galatians participating in (verse 10)?

Read Leviticus 23:33-43

4. Make a few observations of what God commanded His people to observe for the Feast of Booths.

5. What is the LORD's reasoning for celebrating this feast (verse 43)?

6. Why would this not be a requirement today?

In the Law, the LORD gave Moses requirements that included celebrating annual feasts such as the Passover, Booths, and New Moons. When Christ came and died to fulfill the Law, believers were no longer required to participate in these feasts. Remember that the Galatian church had never participated in these anyway because they were not Jewish.

7. Why would the Galatians be attracted to following laws regarding feasts and festivals? Is there something wrong with celebrating?

8. How does Romans 14:5-9 help you reconcile this discussion?

Digging Deeper

Explore Leviticus 23 further. What other feasts and festivals were celebrated? What were the reasons?

Day 3

Read Matthew 5:17-20

9. What does Jesus say He came to do? What do you think this means?

10. How do these verses help you to understand the gospel and what Jesus came to do for you?

11. Since Jesus fulfilled the Law, what is left for you to do?

Paul wanted the Galatians to understand that Jesus was calling His followers to a different kind of quality of righteousness than that of the scribes and Pharisees. The scribes and Pharisees focused on outward activity and appearance.

Review Galatians 4:8-11

12. How does understanding that Jesus is the fulfillment of the Law add to your understanding of Paul's concern that the Galatians should not return to slavery?

Day 4

Reread Galatians 4:8-11

As perplexing as it is that the Galatians would turn to living like slaves, often people really don't want freedom. It seems easier to live according to a list of rules that make your decisions for you. However, Paul warns that what they are returning to is "weak and worthless" (verse 9).

13. Why would he use these particular words?

14. Although church traditions are often done with great intentions, where can you see that we might have similar issues today to Jewish traditions celebrated within the Galatian church?

15. How do you reconcile what Paul is teaching in Galatians with what you think about traditions?

16. Why would Paul say, "I may have labored in vain"?

17. Is there any of these areas that are weak and worthless that you are "holding onto?" What is wrong with "holding onto these?" Is there anything wrong with wanting i.e. to only use the King James Bible?

18. What does holding onto these areas produce in you? Is there something you need to change?

Preferences in the Church Today:

☑ Music style

☑ Bible translations

☑ Passing the offering plate

☑ Pews or chairs

☑ Traditions surrounding communion

☑ Service times/days

☑ Children in the service

Notes

Read 1 Corinthians 10:23-33

Although keeping a perfect Old Testament Law is most likely not our issue today, the principles Paul shares about these areas apply just as much to us as they did to the Galatian church. Where are we holding onto issues that are personal preferences? Where also are we clinging to a conviction even when there is not a specific biblical truth supporting it? Review the chart on the last page of this lesson (10-6) titled *Distinguishing Between Absolutes, Convictions, and Preferences*. Think about issues that you might be holding on to.

19. What do you think about this chart?

20. How do holding onto areas of personal conviction in the church affect our relationship with others?

21. How does God want you to respond to believers whose convictions and preferences differ from yours?

22. What is Paul's conclusion about what is important in verses 31-33?

23. Spend time thinking about yourself and where you might be holding onto areas that are preferences or convictions in your faith. Reflect on your responses and how those affect your ability to reflect the true gospel to others.

DISTINGUISHING BETWEEN ABSOLUTES, CONVICTIONS, AND PREFERENCES

	Absolutes	Convictions	Preferences
D E S C R I P T I O N	*Absolutes* are foundational biblical truths that are so clearly taught in the Scriptures that all believers, regardless of their denominational loyalty or theological perspective, must hold them if they are to be true to the Bible.	*Convictions* are values we have adopted that serve as guidelines for our behavior, either as individuals or as a church. They are personal decisions that shape our conduct and are rooted in absolutes themselves. They are based upon an interpretation of Scripture, an interpretation with which other Christians may or may not agree.	Preferences are choices we make and positions we adopt that are very difficult, if not impossible, to establish from Scripture. They are inclinations based on a number of factors: our personality, our upbringing, our experiences, our current setting.
K E Y S T O I D E N T I F I C A T I O N	• Absolutes have "chapter-and-verse" support. • If a truth is an absolute, it will never change. • Absolutes admit no exceptions. • Absolutes deal primarily with moral principles and internal heart-attitudes, not external actions. • "Any Christian who violates this principle is sinning."	• No chapter and verse can be found for it, but the matter is based on honest interpretation of Scripture. • Godly, Bible-believing Christians disagree on the matter. • If even one exception can be made to it, the issue is conviction and not an absolute. • Convictions primarily address matters of behavior rather than attitudes or moral principles. • "Other Christians may do this, but I can't. To me it is sin."	• Either the Bible does not deal with it at all, or so vaguely that it is impossible to derive any kind of principle from the Scriptures regarding it. • Preferences deal only with personal taste. No moral issue hangs in the balance. • The only justification anyone needs for it is to say, "It's what I personally like." • "I am not sinning if I do it or if I do not do it."

Original information in this table from Dr. Mark Jacobson, Northwest Baptist Seminary

Lesson Eleven
Two Religions

Memory Verse

"More than that, I count all things to be loss because of the surpassing worth of knowing Christ Jesus my Lord."
Philippians 3:8

Paul passionately loved the Galatian church. He realized that it was God who orchestrated that he would end up in the area and gave him the opportunity to share the gospel with these people. And the Galatians were ready for the good news! They received it whole-heartedly! So, when Paul heard that the church had strayed from the message and followed false teachers, you can imagine why he would be perplexed.

Day 1

Read Galatians 4:12-20

1. Give an example from your life or from history where a person was able to lure you or a group of others from the truth.

2. What is different from Paul's tone in this section of the passage?

3. Based on what you have learned about Paul in this study, what does he mean when he says, "become as I am, for I also have become as you are"?

4. What specific differences do you see between Paul's beliefs and those of the Galatian church? How does Philippians 3:7-10 help you to understand this further?

Day 2

| Reread Galatians 4:12-20 |

Reread Galatians 4:12-20. Paul mentions that he preached the gospel in Galatia because of a bodily ailment that caused him to stop in Galatia inadvertently. Scholars are not sure of the exact nature of the ailment although we know it caused great suffering. Read Galatians 4:12-14.

5. Based on this verse, how do you picture Paul when he went to the Galatians? What might your reaction be?

6. Read the following passages. What can you learn about Paul's suffering form each of these passages?

    2 Corinthians 1:3-11

    2 Corinthians 4:7-12

    2 Corinthians 11:23-30

    Colossians 1:24-29

7. Overall, despite Paul's suffering, what did he not lose sight of? Why would he point this out in the letter?

Day 3

8. Over time, the view the Galatians had of Paul had changed. How did the church receive and treat Paul when he first visited them?

9. Why was the fact that he was loved and accepted amazing to Paul?

10. What changed in their attitude toward him?

Day 4

Read Galatians 4:12-20

11. False teachers had infiltrated, flattering the Galatians (verse 17). What are the differences in attitudes and goals between Paul and the other teachers?

Read 2 Peter 2:1-3

12. How does Peter describe the false teachers' ways? What warnings can you gain from this passage?

13. What might be attractive about a false teacher today?

14. Where do you see false teaching today? What does Peter caution to watch out for?

Day 5

Read Luke 18:9-14

In this parable in Luke, Jesus presents a contrast between two men: one who follows a self-righteous religion, and one who responds to the gospel.

15. Describe the two men in the story.

16. Contrast the responses of each of the two men.

17. How does Jesus compare their hearts? What is He looking for?

18. The message of the gospel is so simple, yet often we try to make it so much more. Where do you struggle in this simple message? Where are you like the Pharisee in thinking about all you have done or didn't do in terms of your salvation? Praise God for the simple message of the gospel today!

Lesson Twelve

The Benefits of Obedience

Memory Verse

"So then, brethren, we are not children of a bondwoman, but of the free woman."
Galatians 4:31

Paul continues to contrast law and grace, faith and works, by using the Old Testament story of Abraham as an analogy or illustration of what he had been teaching. Although God promised Abraham a son, he was not given the son right away. As believers, we are promised that we will have struggles and trials in our lives. Jesus tells us in John 16:33, "In the world, you will have trouble." Peter explains we are not to be "surprised at the fiery trial when it comes upon you to test you."

Although we are to expect hardship and suffering, we are often caught off guard when something doesn't go the way we have anticipated. Like Abraham, it is easy to take matters into our own hands.

Day 1

God promised Abraham a son, and many years later Sarah, his wife, still had not conceived. According to the traditions of the day, if he did not have a son, then Eliezer of Damascus, his chief servant, would be his heir. God reaffirmed his original promise to Abraham and told him the son would be from his own body (Genesis 15:1-4). Sarah was frustrated, however, and convinced Abraham to father a child by a female slave, Hagar, which would then be considered hers. Instead of waiting in faith for God to provide, they chose their own solution.

Read Genesis 16:1-16

1. Describe a time you got something you wanted but it turned out to be more of a burden than you anticipated.

2. What circumstances surrounded the birth of Ishmael?

3. What do these circumstances reveal about the heart of Sarah and Abraham?

4. Describe the kind of man Ishmael would become (16:12)?

5. What does James 1:14-15 teach about the consequences of neglecting God's ways?

6. Read the following verses. What results from the neglect of God's ways?

   1 John 2:4-6

   Ephesians 4:26-27

   James 1:22-24

7. Are you experiencing these results? Why would this look like slavery? Where might you be neglecting God's ways?

Day 2

Read Genesis 21:1-7

8. What circumstances surround the birth of Isaac?

9. What can you learn about the character of God through this story?

10. How does this story differ from the birth of Ishmael?

Day 3

Read Galatians 4:21-31

In the next section of Galatians, Paul takes the opportunity to contrast the choices of Abraham. The birth of Ishmael through Hagar was "according to the flesh." This was a choice motivated by selfish desires since Abraham and Sarah chose to solve their own problem of lacking an heir. This selfish choice resulted in consequences that were destructive. In contrast, the birth of Isaac was completed supernaturally "through the promise." When Isaac was born, Sarah and Abraham were physically too old to have children. Isaac's birth demonstrates God's miraculous provision and fulfills His promise to provide Abraham with a son.

11. From Galatians 4:21-31, list the characteristics of the two covenants.

OLD COVENANT	NEW COVENANT

Which covenant do the following people represent: The Old or New Covenant?

Sarah _____

Hagar _____

Ishmael _____

Isaac _____

12. The Galatian church was struggling. They thought they needed to live by both covenants. Why wouldn't this be possible (verse 31)?

Day 4

Digging Deeper

Look up verses that contain God's promises to you. Make a "Promise Journal" recording the promises you find. Use your "Promise Journal" as a quick reference for those times when you need the encouragement that comes from claiming God's promises.

---

13. What declarations are made about the one who is born of the free woman (Galatians 4:28-31)?

14. What is the significance of Paul's instructions in verse 30? (Review Genesis 21:10; the first time these words were used.)

15. What areas and/or activities in your life need to be "cast out" because they are a result of law and not born out of your freedom in Christ?

16. Like Sarah, in what area of your life are you tempted to run ahead of God and take matters into your own hands?

17. Instead of taking matters into your own hands and living like a slave, what hope do the following verses give you?

Ephesians 4:22-32

Colossians 3:5-17

James 1:22-25

18. Why would living an obedient life to God provide freedom?

Day 5

Read Psalm 73

Can you truly say like David, "There is nothing on earth I desire besides you"? God desires us to live a life of freedom. However, when we do things our own way, we don't experience the peace, joy and security that we have when we live a life obedient to Christ.

19. In what areas of your life do you desire to live out the freedom God has provided for you?

20. Reflect on the contrasted emotions in this psalm of a life lived out of obedience to the living God and a life lived in obedience.

21. What blessings are provided to the one that lives in obedience?

22. What promise from this psalm encourages you today?

Lesson Thirteen

Does God Really Love Me?

Although circumcision is mentioned previously in this letter, Paul addresses the issue of circumcision directly in this section. Remember, the book of Galatians is written to the Galatian churches that consisted of Gentile believers. Since they weren't Jews, they had never been under the Old Testament laws, including the law that required males to be circumcised.

In this passage, Paul clarifies that we are no longer bound by the demands of the Old Testament Law. If someone were required to keep a part of the Law such as circumcision, then they would be required to keep the entire Old Testament Law, thus making what Christ did on the cross unnecessary. Complete adherence to the Law was not God's plan for humanity because He knows that we cannot keep the Law perfectly. However, we continually forget this and add obedience to the Law as a means of obtaining God's love, forgetting about God's free gift of salvation through the cross.

Day 1

1. Recall a time you learned something in theory and then had to try it in reality.

Read Galatians 5:1-6
---

2. Galatians 5:1 summarizes the theme of the book. Look up the verse in a few different versions of the Bible and write it out in your own words.

3. According to Galatians 5:1, in what ways are believers to respond to their freedom?

4. What areas can be "enslaving" to believers, or in other words, what can keep believers from enjoying the freedom they have in Christ?

Digging Deeper

Review Galatians 2:11-16.
What area was Peter struggling with in this passage?

Who was being led astray? Why?

Why is it important to be aware of how our actions affect others?

Day 2

Read Galatians 5:1-6

Remember the Old Testament Law requires full obedience. In this section, we see the Galatians picking and choosing which laws will justify or, in other words, make them right before God.

5. Beginning in verse 2, Paul makes several arguments to rebut the justification of circumcision. What arguments from Paul do you find in this passage?

6. It is impossible to save ourselves or do anything in order to earn God's favor. What does Galatians 2:16 tell us about how we are justified?

7. Read Ephesians 2:8-9 and 2 Timothy 1:9. How do these verses support what Paul is writing about to the Galatians?

The Galatians believed circumcision was a way to attain and keep God's approval and love. It may not be something that is a challenge for us today; however, many women continually look for ways to maintain love and approval with God. Sometimes these are very subtle. For one woman, it might be avoiding R-rated movies or allowing her children to only play with kids from church. If she keeps this standard, then she has maintained God's approval and love.

8. What subtle ways might women try to maintain God's approval?

9. Think about your own views of the gospel. What do you believe regarding what you must do to earn your salvation? What about maintaining God's love and approval?

10. How do you reconcile these beliefs with the verses from questions 6 and 7?

Read Galatians 5:1-6

11. What were the Galatians not to return to (verse 1)?

12. Contrast the yoke of slavery, mentioned in Acts 15:10-11, with the yoke Jesus provides (Matthew 11:28-30).

YOKE OF SLAVERY	YOKE OF JESUS

13. Describe the life of one that has put on the yoke of slavery and contrast it with what a life would look like which has put on the yoke of Jesus.

14. Take time to evaluate your own life. Consider which yoke you most often put on.

Jesus has paid the full price for you by dying on the cross for your sin. Because you could not do anything for salvation, He did it all through the sacrificial death of His Son on the cross.

15. What truths do Romans 8:3 have for the one who is putting on the yoke of slavery?

16. What verse might you use to encourage someone to put on the yoke of Jesus?

Read Galatians 5:1-6

17. Verse 5:4 says, "You are severed from Christ, you who would be justified by the law; you have fallen away from grace" (ESV). *Severed* means to nullify the effect. What would happen if Paul's warnings were ignored? What might that look like in the life of a believer?

18. What characterizes a life of faith lived in freedom (verses 5-6)?

The evidence of a life that knows it is saved by grace alone is one of faith working through love. This means that recognizing the love that Christ has for you, which is demonstrated through the gospel, will enable you to love God and others freely. The gospel is a model of what love is and how we can love. This is the first mention of love in the book of Galatians and will be a new theme through the remainder of the book.

19. What might a believer's life look like when they are living a life in response to God's love?

20. In what ways is your life characterized by:

Love

Rules and regulations

What adjustments need to be made?

Read Psalm 78

This passage is a call of God's people to His redemptive love, and Israel refuses to accept it.

21. Compare and contrast Israel's disobedience with God's love and provision for His people. What can you learn about God's redemptive love from this passage?

22. How does this encourage you? How does this motivate you?

Psalm 78 is a picture of Israel's refusal to accept God's love. It is also a picture of how God delights to shower His favor upon those who humbly accept it. We have a difficult time accepting this and continue to strive in our efforts. Jesus paid the full price for our sin by dying so that we can live in freedom. It becomes so exhausting when we try desperately to gain His love and approval by creating our own laws. Although today, circumcision may not be our issue, there are so many other ways we try to earn God's love and approval. Thankfully, through Christ and His redemptive work on the cross, we have the freedom to live free. In turn, we can rest in the yoke of Jesus.

23. Do you believe God loves you? How do you respond to His love?

24. Write a prayer admitting to God where you are not living free in Christ's love. Express thanksgiving for the freedom Christ has provided you by dying on the cross.

Lesson Fourteen
Running Well

Memory Verse

"A little leaven leavens the whole lump of dough."
Galatians 5:9

Recall Psalm 78 from last week. Can you remember how God's people had strayed from His sovereign grace and plan? God called His people to listen to His Word (78:1-7). Again and again they didn't want to listen to God and chose not to follow his ways. While God was just, He also was continuously loving and compassionate and continued to direct His people back to the right path. The Galatian church was also off track. They had bought into something different and left behind the pure, simple gospel. Today is no different; we can easily be people that get off track from the truth of His Word.

Day 1

1. Recall a recent instance when your day started off well but then became very hectic. What happened?

> **Read Galatians 5:7-12**

2. The Galatians had been running well. Paul often uses the analogy of running a race for living the Christian life. Look up the following passages and record the characteristics involved in "running well."

PASSAGE	CHARACTERISTICS OF RUNNING WELL
1 Cor 9:24-27	
Phil 2:16	
2 Tim 4:7	
Heb 12:1	
Any Others	

3. In what ways are the characteristics of running well absent from the Galatian church? Use specific examples.

4. What impacts you from this list in question 2? How might you evaluate how you run through this list?

Day 2

Read Galatians 5:7-12

The Galatians had accepted the gospel and were running well. Paul now asks, "Who hindered you from obeying the truth?" Apparently there had been a leader of the false teachers who had greatly impacted and swayed the church from the gospel they had learned.

5. Paul points out a person (probably a leader of false teachers) that was a hindrance to the people's obedience. In what ways can others become a hindrance that keep a person from running well? How do you see this today? Is there someone or something that is hindering you from obedience?

6. Instead of relying on the wisdom of the world, yourself, or others, where should a believer go for answers?

7. Read Hebrews 4:12. Describe the Word of God from this verse and how it will help someone to run well.

8. In your own life, where does God's Word fit in? How could it make a difference in running well?

Read Galatians 5:7-12

When baking, leaven is added to make bread rise. Only a small amount of leaven is needed to permeate through the entire dough. Many times in the Bible, leaven is used as a symbol of how a small amount of something can have a great, unseen effect. In the Old Testament, God's people would get rid of any leaven that they had in the house during the Feast of Unleavened Bread to remember God's gracious redemption of His people from slavery (Exodus 12:17). Paul uses the illustration of leavened bread in Galatians to further explain the powerful influences false teachers had that hindered the church. Jesus Himself uses the example of the leavened bread in Luke 12:1-3 regarding the Pharisees.

Read Luke 12:1-3

9. What is Jesus' warning in this passage?

10. What is His reason for the warning?

Read Luke 11:42-44

11. What can you learn about the Pharisees from this passage?

12. How does this context better help you understand the leaven in Jesus' warning?

What a great example of how easy it is to be sidetracked from the truth. A little bit of something can get us really off track. The Galatians were buying into a whole new list of rules that they needed to maintain in order to be loved and accepted by God.

13. Is there any "leaven" or false teaching in your own life that involves keeping certain rules and standards (not based on God's Word) in order to be more accepted by God? Consider the list to the side of areas where we have the potential struggle.

Digging Deeper

Feasts in the Old Testament gave God's people a chance to reflect on who God is. Read Exodus 12:14-20 and 13:3-10 about the Feast of Unleavened Bread. What is God trying to teach His people by having them refrain from eating leaven for seven days? What can you learn from this Old Testament feast about the character of God?

Day 4

Read 1 Corinthians 5:6-8

14. What are believers encouraged to do with the leaven we have allowed into our lives (verses 6-7)?

15. According to this passage, how are we, as believers, already viewed (verse 7)?

I think God should love and accept me because...

☑ I have obeyed enough.

☑ I am the perfect homemaker.

☑ I make homemade meals every night.

☑ I don't pursue any activities that do not involve my children or husband.

☑ I don't disagree with people — especially my husband.

☑ I only home school my children.

☑ I vote a certain way.

☑ I boycott places that support gay rights.

☑ When my children misbehave, I can quote verses to them.

☑ I only read Christian books and listen only to Christian music.

☑ I don't say no when someone makes a request of me.

☑ I am at church every time the doors are open.

16. What is the hope offered in this passage for cleansing out the leaven in our lives (verse 7b)?

17. What hope does this bring you personally?

Just as God delivered the Israelites out of a land full of corruption, He delivers His people from the bond of slavery and into freedom through Christ's death on the cross. Christ already sees us as people that are "unleavened" because of His great sacrifice, which is a great reason for celebration.

Read Galatians 5:12

Paul wraps up his plea with a harsh illustration. If Paul was preaching circumcision, then why was he being persecuted?

18. Why does Paul use such a harsh illustration in verse 12?

19. How does this illustration impact you?

Day 5

We must be careful to be wise about the false teaching that can slowly creep into our thinking. Paul took this seriously, and so should we. Whether this comes from the world, others, or ourselves, we need to go to God's Word in order to find the truth. Even a little amount of untruth in our lives can lead us away from God's best for our lives. Psalm 119 is a reminder that the written Word of God is a gift to His people.

Meditate on Psalm 119 today and record all that God's Word provides.

How does this list encourage you?

Lesson Fifteen
True Freedom

Memory Verse

"Therefore we have been buried with Him by baptism into death, so that as Christ was raised from the dead through the glory of the Father, so we too might walk in newness of life."
Romans 6:4

In 1863, when slaves were emancipated in the United States, sadly, some continued to live under the control of their master. Many of these slaves, although granted freedom, did not know how to live a life as anything other than a slave. How would you feel watching a freed slave continue to live in slavery? That's how Satan wants you to live. He wants to convince you that the gospel didn't really free you; you are still guilty and will never be able to live without your old slave ways. Do you truly understand and appreciate the freedom the gospel provides?

Day 1

1. Imagine yourself in 1863 watching the free man continue to live as a slave. What could you tell him about freedom?

Jesus proclaimed in John 8:36, "so if the son sets you free, you will be free indeed." Jesus has set us free from the chains of sin. We no longer remain under its life-controlling power. We have been set free!

Read Galatians 5:13-15

2. What is the freedom we have been called to?

3. What warning is given in regards to this freedom?

We are called to a life of freedom—freedom from sin and from trying to earn God's love and acceptance by keeping a list of rules. However, freedom is in no way to become an excuse for indulging the flesh; in other words, pursuing self-gratifying desires. Our desires can start off pure, but we can easily get off track, and then our desires can become self-gratifying. Our freedom was not given so we can pursue our own desires, but rather given to pursue loving God and others.

4. List ways freedom can become an opportunity to live out self-gratifying desires.

5. What encouragement does Galatians 2:20-21 give you as you look back at your list?

Digging Deeper

Look further at the words of Jesus in John 8:31-38. What further insights can you gain about freedom?

Notes

15-2

Day 2

Paul gives further instructions on how we can exercise our freedom and keep from carrying out our self-gratifying desires, referred to as our flesh.

Read Romans 6:1-14 (ESV)
---

[1]What shall we say then? Are we to continue in sin that grace may abound? [2]By no means! How can we who died to sin still live in it? [3]Do you not know that all of us who have been baptized into Christ Jesus were baptized into his death? [4]We were buried therefore with him by baptism into death, in order that, just as Christ was raised from the dead by the glory of the Father, we too might walk in newness of life. [5]For if we have been united with him in a death like his, we shall certainly be united with him in a resurrection like his. [6]We know that our old self [a] was crucified with him in order that the body of sin might be brought to nothing, so that we would no longer be enslaved to sin. [7]For one who has died has been set free[b] from sin. [8]Now if we have died with Christ, we believe that we will also live with him. [9]We know that Christ, being raised from the dead, will never die again; death no longer has dominion over him. [10]For the death he died he died to sin, once for all, but the life he lives he lives to God. [11]So you also must consider yourselves dead to sin and alive to God in Christ Jesus. [12]Let not sin therefore reign in your mortal body, to make you obey its passions. [13]Do not present your members to sin as instruments for unrighteousness, but present yourselves to God as those who have been brought from death to life, and your members to God as instruments for righteousness. [14]For sin will have no dominion over you, since you are not under law but under grace.

6. Circle the word "know" in this passage. What three truths are we to know?

Baptism...

In this passage, it is not referring to water baptism. Instead it means: "to identify with."

"[13]You, my brothers and sisters, were called to be free. But do not use your freedom to indulge the flesh [a]; rather, serve one another humbly in love."
Galatians 5:13 (NIV)

7. What declarations does Paul make about sin's control in our lives?

8. How do these truths affect your attitude toward living in victory over sin?

Day 3

Reread Romans 6:1-14

9. What contrast does Paul make in verse 11?

10. How does a physically dead person respond to things happening around him? How does this relate to sin?

11. Go back to the Romans 6:1-14 passage. Put a box around the word "consider."

12. How does considering yourself dead to sin help you resist desires of your flesh?

13. How should that affect your everyday life? Consider your relationships, your responses to others?

Day 4

Reread Romans 6:1-14

Because God has brought us from death to life, we are not obligated to sin anymore. Everyday we can present ourselves to God with every part of our body: hands, feet, eyes, minds, voices and ears. Our bodies that were once full of sin are now instruments for righteousness.

14. Underline the word "present" in this passage.

15. What two options do we have in what we present to God?

16. What makes it possible to present ourselves as an instrument of righteousness (verse 13)?

17. What specific differences would it make in your life if you woke up every morning realizing you were no longer chained to sin and under its control, but instead identified with Christ and His power to live victoriously?

18. Read Galatians 5:13-15 again. How does the truth of Romans 6:1-14 help you to follow Paul's instruction of living in freedom but not using it as an opportunity for the flesh?

Day 5

Christ provided great freedom from the chains of sin and the obligation to rules and regulations. Romans 6:14 says, "For sin will have no dominion over you, since you are not under law but under grace." As we answer our call to freedom and desire to present ourselves as instruments of righteousness, thoughtfully consider and read 2 Peter 1:3-11.

19. What are the promises in 2 Peter 1:3-4?

20. Paul says in verse 8, "these qualities are yours and increasing." What qualities do we already possess in Christ (verse 5-7)?

21. If we lack these qualities, what have we forgotten (verse 9)?

22. What encouragement do these verses give us to live in freedom?

Lesson Sixteen
Loving Others

Memory Verse

"Therefore we have been buried with Him by baptism into death, so that as Christ was raised from the dead through the glory of the Father, so we too might walk in newness of life."
Romans 6:4

All of us are tempted to live for our selfish desires. But no matter what temptation we might be facing at the moment, our selfish lives of slavery are now dead because of the gospel. We have all the resources of Christ available to live a life of righteousness.

In this freedom, it is not enough just to recognize the power to say no to our fleshly desires. We are called instead to love others. The gospel enables us to have that love for others out of the same love Christ demonstrated for us.

Day 1

1. When have you recently seen an example of someone lovingly serving another?

Read Galatians 5:13-15

2. Rather than living for our desires and ourselves, what does this passage tell us we should be doing?

3. In what ways would fleshly desires hinder someone from loving and serving others?

Notes

4. What does Jesus tell us in this passage about what we must do?

The cross is a symbol of following Christ. This means you are to put aside your needs and desires and instead follow Christ's desires.

5. Where do you need to deny yourself (your own fleshly desires) and instead take up the cross of Jesus?

Day 2

Paul calls us to flee from our fleshly desires and in turn follow Christ through lovingly serving one another. This means taking the focus off ourselves in daily situations and relationships and regarding others as more important than our own desires.

6. What daily situations and relationships are you tempted to regard yourself and your own desires as more important?

Read Philippians 2:3-11

7. How did Paul instruct us to love others (verses 3-4)?

8. How did Jesus demonstrate what it meant to be a servant?

9. How does this passage impact your thoughts on lovingly serving others?

10. What could you do differently in the situation you mentioned in question 7?

Day 3

In the Book of Genesis, man and woman were created in God's image. This means you were created to be like God. Ephesians 5:1 says, "Therefore be imitators of God, as beloved children. And walk in love, as Christ loved us and gave himself up for us, a fragrant offering of sacrifice to God" (ESV). God is a God of love. When we love, we are behaving how we were created. When we are living in the flesh and focusing on our own fleshly desires, we take our focus off of serving God and others. Contentment and joy come from an obedient response to the way we were created.

Read Matthew 22:37-39

11. What are the two commands given in this passage?

12. What does love demonstrate?

13. How is it possible to love others?

14. What do you learn about your love for others?

15. What is a current situation where it is difficult for you to love someone?

16. How will understanding Christ's love help you to have the same love for that person?

Love...

"Love is willing self-sacrifice for the good of another that does not require reciprocation or that the person being loved is deserving."
(Paul Tripp, *What Did You Expect?*, p. 188)

Digging Deeper

Read Romans 14:13-15:3 for an explanation of love when believers have differing views. In the following chart, record what love does and what love does not do.

WHAT LOVE DOES	WHAT LOVE DOES NOT DO

What conclusion can you draw from this passage?

Day 4

Paul concludes this section with a sarcastic statement in an attempt to make a strong point.

> **Read Galatians 5:13-15**

17. When you are not motivated by a heart that lovingly serves others, what are the results?

18. What can't the law can accomplish in relationships with others?

19. How would fulfilling the one law of loving your neighbor as yourself restore relationships?

Day 5

> **Read 1 Corinthians 13:1-8**

1 Corinthians 13 is a popular passage describing love. Many think of love as simply being an emotion, but love requires action such as being patient, kind, not envying, not boasting, not being rude, and keeping no record of wrong.

What aspect of love in 1 Corinthians 13:1-8 do you have the opportunity to apply in your life?

Write a prayer thanking God for His love for us and for giving us the means to love others in the same way.

Lesson Seventeen

Walking by the Spirit

Memory Verse

"But I say, walk by the Spirit, and you will not carry out the desire of the flesh. For the flesh sets its desire against the Spirit, and the Spirit against the flesh"
Galatians 5:16-17a

Because of the finished work on the cross, believers have been set free from the bondage of sin and have been set free to follow and obey God. But how do we do this? How can we experience victory over our flesh?

Day 1

> **Read Galatians 5:16-26**

1. What is the command in verse 16?

2. What are the results of obedience?

3. Describe the conflict recorded in this passage.

4. Why is this conflict unique to believers?

5. In the chart below, write down all you learn about the flesh and the Spirit from this passage?

THE FLESH	THE SPIRIT

6. Why is it impossible for the flesh and Spirit to work together?

7. How does the promise in verse 16 give you hope?

Day 2

Because it is impossible for the flesh and the Spirit to work together, Christians face an ongoing battle. At any given time, we either give control to our sinful nature, or we yield to the control of the Holy Spirit. We continually have a choice to make: Live for our own selfish desires, or yield to what God wants for us. Romans 7 provides insight into the war between the flesh and the Holy Spirit. Paul writes about his personal battle with his flesh.

Read Romans 7:13-25

8. Make a list of the struggles Paul has in this passage.

9. In what circumstances in your own life do you identify with Paul?

10. When are you most likely to follow your own desires?

11. What is true when you desire God's will over your own?

12. What causes Paul to give thanks in the midst of the battle?

13. Why should the gospel be a source of hope for you in the conflict between the flesh and Spirit?

Day 3

Walking by the Spirit is being led by the Spirit. At salvation, the Holy Spirit indwells each believer. He is sent to guide, direct, and encourage us. His leading will direct us to obedience and will always be in agreement with the Word of God. When we allow the Spirit to guide and lead us, we will not choose to indulge our fleshly desires. Even though the conflict between the flesh and the Spirit is intense and ongoing, God has provided a path of victory. If we just try to manage our flesh and "keep it under control," we will fail. But if we "walk by the Spirit," we will enjoy the freedom that is ours because of Christ.

Read Galatians 5:16-18

14. When you think of someone being led, what do you picture?

15. How does that picture help you understand what the Holy Spirit does for you?

16. If you allow fleshly desires to lead you, what will result?

Walk...

In the New Testament, the word "walk" usually refers to a person's conduct, pattern of lifestyle or overall direction of one's life. In other places in Scripture, the picture of walking is translated as "in the Spirit," "according to the Spirit," or "to be filled with the Spirit."

17. How have you experienced the Holy Spirit's leading in your own life?

18. What was the result?

Day 4

Walking by the Spirit isn't just about doing the right thing. Learning to walk by the Spirit involves our minds. How we think will determine the choices we make and the behavior we show.

| Read Romans 8:5-8 |

19. For someone whose mind is filled with selfish desires, what results can be expected?

20. What things would fall under the category of thinking about "things of the Spirit?"

21. Read Romans 12:2. What is the result of having one's mind renewed and transformed by truth?

22. How would right thinking affect your ability to allow the Holy Spirit to lead you?

The Holy Spirit...

☑ Convicts (John 16:8-11)

☑ Illuminates (John 16:12-15)

☑ Teaches (John 16:12-15)

☑ Guides (Romans 8:14)

☑ Assures (Romans 8:16)

☑ Intercedes (Romans 8:26)

☑ Directs (Acts 20:22)

☑ Warns (Acts 20:23)

Digging Deeper

Use a concordance or www.biblegateway.com to find other verses about the mind. What verses did you find? What insights did you gain?

Study the sidebar. Philippians 4:8 outlines how a believer should focus their thinking.

Read Psalms 19:7-9

23. What descriptions are used for God's Word?

24. How do Psalm 19 and Philippians 4 compare?

25. What significance does the Word of God play in learning how to walk by the Spirit?

Day 5

Read Galatians 5:16-18

Living by the flesh always results in more fleshly living. It will never lead to righteousness. On the other hand, when believers practice walking by the Spirit, it leads to a greater sensitivity and a desire to continue to follow and obey.

"Finally brethren, whatever is true, whatever is honorable, whatever is right, whatever is pure, whatever is lovely, whatever is of good repute, if there is any excellence and if anything worthy of praise, dwell on these things."
Philippians 4:8 (NASB)

Even though the conflict between the flesh and Spirit is intense and ongoing, God has provided a path of victory. If we just try to manage our flesh and "keep it under control," we will fail. But if we "walk by the Spirit," we will enjoy the freedom that is ours because of Christ.

26. If you are walking by the Spirit, why is the Law no longer necessary?

27. How can you cooperate with God's desire to teach you to "walk by the Spirit?"

28. Review your answer to the study from Day 1. In the midst of this battle between the flesh and the Spirit, what can you praise God for?

Lesson Eighteen

Experiencing Freedom
The Ability to Obey

We have learned that freedom comes from a relationship with Christ. This relationship is not based on rules and regulations, like the Law, but it is based on faith in the finished work of Christ on the cross. And the freedom believers enjoy is not freedom to live out their own desires and passion. True Christian freedom is enjoyed when believers understand that they have been set free from the bondage of sin and have been given the ability to obey God and enjoy fellowship with Him.

There is still a conflict. Our old nature does not just disappear at salvation. Believers still have the flesh to contend with. But believers cannot fight against the flesh on their own power. As we learned in the previous lesson, the Spirit of God enables us to say no to the flesh and yes to godly living.

But what is the flesh? What is the Spirit up against? What does the flesh look like in everyday life?

Day 1

Quoting Old Testament passages, Paul describes the condition of every human heart left to itself. Read the following passage from Romans carefully. Remember, we all start out this way.

Romans 3:10-19 (NASB)
[10]as it is written,
"THERE IS NONE RIGHTEOUS, NOT EVEN ONE;
[11]THERE IS NONE WHO UNDERSTANDS,
THERE IS NONE WHO SEEKS GOD;
[12]ALL HAVE TURNED ASIDE, TOGETHER THEY HAVE BECOME USELESS; THERE IS NONE WHO DOES GOOD,
THERE IS NOT EVEN ONE."
[13]"THEIR THROAT IS AN OPEN GRAVE,

WITH THEIR TONGUES THEY KEEP DECEIVING,"
"THE POISON OF ASPS IS UNDER THEIR LIPS";
[14]"WHOSE MOUTH IS FULL OF CURSING AND BITTERNESS";
[15]"THEIR FEET ARE SWIFT TO SHED BLOOD,
[16]DESTRUCTION AND MISERY ARE IN THEIR PATHS,
[17]AND THE PATH OF PEACE THEY HAVE NOT KNOWN."
[18]"THERE IS NO FEAR OF GOD BEFORE THEIR EYES."

1. Underline the words that show amount. Why is this significant?

2. What areas of life are affected by the flesh? What does a fleshly heart lack?

3. How does this passage impact you?

This is the condition of the heart when Christ reaches down and rescues someone. Romans 5:8 tells us that "God shows His love for us in that while we were still sinners, Christ died for us." You and I have no ability on our own to change our hearts or defeat the flesh in our lives. Faith in Christ's finished work on the cross is our only hope for life-transforming change. And even after salvation, if we yield to our flesh and refuse the help of the Spirit, we can head down a very wrong path.

Day 2

Fleshly living is selfish living. When a person makes choices and decisions based on their own passions and desires, the results do not lead to righteous living. Remember that the flesh and the Spirit produce opposite results in our lives. Living for the flesh does not bring freedom; it returns a believer to bondage.

> **Read Galatians 5:19-21**

Area #1—SEXUAL PASSIONS
(Galatians 5:19)

- Immorality = Any sexual activity outside of marriage.
- Impurity = Sexual deviations, including homosexuality (this includes all types of pornography).
- Sensuality = Sexual deviations of the grossest kind (including shocking acts of indecency).

Area #2—RELIGIOUS PASSIONS

- Idolatry = Worship and adoration of created things.
- Sorcery = Religious and superstitious practices that exclude the total authority of Scripture.

Area #3 – SOCIAL EMOTIONAL EXCESS

- Enmities = An attitude of hostility.
- Strife = An argumentative and quarrelsome attitude.
- Jealousy = A bitter and envious resentment attitude.
- Outbursts of anger = Hot tempered reactions that cause pain for others.
- Disputes = An attitude of rivalry and opposition.
- Dissensions = An undue promotion of personal opinions.
- Factions = Cliques that destroy unity and ministry.
- Envying = Hostility resulting from prolonged jealousy.
- Drunkenness = Loss of control and human senses and reasoning ability.
- Carousing = Parties of drunkenness and illicit sexual activity.

4. What are your initial thoughts as you read this list?

5. What does the phrase, "...and things like these..." in verse 21 indicate about this list?

6. Why is that important to understand?

Study the sidebar to the left.

7. What areas of life can be affected by the flesh?

8. How does it impact you to realize that, in your flesh, you are capable of choosing any of these wrong behaviors?

9. In what circumstances are you tempted to respond in the flesh? What are the results?

10. Why will living out the flesh never result in righteousness?

11. What is Paul's warning to those who do not turn from their fleshly desires (see note in sidebar)?

Sin...

Paul is not talking about the "act" of sin but a "habit" of sin. Paul clearly states that even those who sin in these ways can have their lives changed by Christ. However, those who say they are Christians but persist in a continual, habitual practice of sin with no evidence of repentance will not inherit the kingdom of God. Such people need to re-evaluate their lives to see if they truly believe and understand the gospel.

12. Read the following passages. What do they reveal about the real root of fleshly living?

    Matthew 12:33-35

    Matthew 15:18-19

    Luke 6:43-45

13. What is filling your heart when you yield to your own selfish desires?

14. Why are rules and regulations (like the Law) ineffective in curbing fleshly responses?

15. How have you experienced this in your own life?

What comes out of a sponge when it gets squeezed? Whatever it has been soaking in. The same is true for people. Whatever saturates our heart and mind is what will come out of us.

Read Romans 8:5-8

16. Fill in the chart.

CHARACTERISTICS OF A FLESHLY MINDSET	CHARACTERISTICS OF A SPIRIT-FILLED MINDSET

17. What are the results of a fleshly mindset?

18. What do your responses and choices reveal about what you are allowing to fill your mind?

19. What changes can you make to fill your mind with things of the Spirit?

Day 4

Read Colossians 3:1-15. In this passage, the "old self" refers to the flesh. The term "new self" describes a believer's new nature that is given at salvation.

20. Record what you learn about the old self and new self from this passage.

OLD SELF	NEW SELF

21. According to verses 1-3, why is it possible for these fleshly characteristics to be absent from a believer's life?

22. How does remembering a believer's position in Christ encourage them to think rightly about their flesh?

Verse 5 tells us to "consider the members of your earthly body as dead..." In this passage, the word "consider" carries the idea of acting as if it were so. "Considering" is an act of faith because it requires that you believe what is true even though your feelings might tell you otherwise. For the believer, it is a fact that Christ's finished work on the cross crucified sin's authority in their life. The flesh is very powerful, but it is also a fact that the indwelling Holy Spirit has been given to empower a believer to say no to self and yes to godliness.

23. How do your feelings about the flesh and sin in your own life cloud your ability to believe the truth?

24. Why is it important to remember the truth of the gospel in this conflict with the flesh?

25. What do your responses in life (fleshly or Spirit-led) reveal about what you believe?

26. What truth do you need to remember in order for you to "consider the members of your earthly body as dead..."?

Day 5

> **Review Galatians 5:16-26**

27. What can we be assured of if we walk by the Spirit?

28. What changes would occur in your life if you followed this command and believed the promise that comes with it?

29. How can you cooperate with God's plan to overcome the flesh in your life?

30. Write a prayer of thanksgiving to the Lord, thanking Him for the work of the Spirit in your life.

Notes

Lesson Nineteen
The Fruit of the Spirit

Memory Verse
"But the fruit of the Spirit is love, joy, peace, patience, kindness, goodness, faithfulness, gentleness, self-control; against such things there is no law. Now those who belong to Christ Jesus have crucified the flesh with its passions and desires. If we live by the Spirit, let us also walk by the Spirit."
Galatians 5:22-25

With the Holy Spirit's power and help, we are able to take off the old self with its fleshly pursuits. Paul doesn't leave the Galatians in this spot but goes on to say what the true evidence of the Holy Spirit is: the presence of the fruit of the Spirit in the believer's life. We are free from bondage and slavery to sin through Christ's death on the cross, and with that, we're free to walk by the Spirit and bear fruit.

Day 1

Read Galatians 5:22-25

1. Make a list of the fruit of the Spirit.

2. Who produces the fruit?

3. Verse 22 begins with a contrast. What is Paul contrasting the fruit of the Spirit with?

4. Why is it important to understand that these two lists are opposite?

5. How does this encourage you in regards to your potential as a believer?

Digging Deeper

Compare the list of the characteristics in 2 Peter 1:5-8 with the fruit of the Spirit. What further insight do you gain?

Day 2

The fruit of the Spirit grows in the life of a believer no differently than the fruit we enjoy to eat grows on a vine. Jesus explained this principle to His disciples in John 15.

Read John 15:4-5, 8

The word "abiding" in this passage has the idea of close personal relationships. In the physical world, a branch of a fruit-bearing tree is attached to a larger trunk that supplies it with life-giving nutrients. Without this continuous relationship, no fruit will grow on the branch. In our spiritual lives, the same is true. If a believer is not experiencing a growing, close walk with the Lord, fruit will not be evident.

6. What is true of the branch that is bearing fruit in this passage?

7. What does the presence of fruit indicate to a believer and those watching?

8. What things tend to interrupt a close, growing relationship with the Lord?

9. How can you make yourself available to stay connected to "the Vine"?

- LOVE = A clear choice to actively seek and do God's best for someone, regardless of the treatment received from that person. This love is unconditional, sacrificial and supernatural.

- JOY = An internal satisfaction and pleasure that is always obvious to others.

- PEACE = A state of mind free from fear, worry, and agitation, allowing harmony with Jesus Christ to exist.

- PATIENCE = The ability to react calmly to the unjust situations of life, without getting angry.

- KINDNESS = Putting others at ease in your presence, being careful to not inflict the pain of degrading.

- GOODNESS = Being generous to others with an open-handed, open-hearted approach.

- FAITHFULNESS = Loyal reliability that allows a person to build a reputation of dependability and trustworthiness.

- GENTLENESS = A controlled reaction to others, which combines strength and tenderness. It allows you to choose your response to people rather than simply reacting to them.

- SELF-CONTROL = Proper restraint over bodily appetites and the desirous will.

Day 3

Jesus sent His Spirit to dwell in believers to produce Himself in us. His life is characterized by the fruit of the Spirit in the midst of a world where the opposite is seen so clearly. Heaven is not the sole benefit of salvation. God is in the business of changing His children to look more like His Son. This supernatural process of heart transformation is called sanctification. If believers live by the power of the Holy Spirit, we will bear Christ's characteristics.

| Read Galatians 5:22-23 |

10. Notice that the word "fruit" is singular. Why is that significant?

11. How are the "parts" of the fruit connected?

12. How have you seen this in your own life?

13. If you are yielding to the Spirit and bearing fruit, why are rules and regulations unnecessary?

Day 4

| Read Galatians 3:1-3 |

14. Why is Paul scolding the Galatians?

15. Why is this a foolish pursuit?

16. How are you tempted to grow and change on your own?

17. What are the results in your life?

We are called to bear fruit, not produce it. We can cooperate with the Holy Spirit or work against Him. On our own, we can only produce deeds of the flesh from our own power. Remember the example of John 15 ... The branch does not work hard to produce the fruit. It remains connected to the vine. The same is true for believers.

> **Read Galatians 5:24-25**

18. What is true of those who belong to Christ Jesus?

19. Notice that the verb "have crucified" is past tense. Why is it significant that this has already happened?

20. What do your choices look like when you forget that you don't have to yield to selfish temptations?

21. How does reminding yourself of Christ's work in your life help you cooperate with His plan for producing fruit in your life?

Perfected...

The word translated "perfected" in Galatians 3:3 means "matured" or "to be completed."

As Christians, we still have the capacity to sin, but we have been set free from its power over us and no longer have to give into the flesh. Without the Spirit's presence and power, the only choice we can make is to live according to our own fleshly desires. But for those who know Christ, we have another choice. We can continually surrender our sinful tendencies to God's control and draw upon the Spirit's power to overcome them. The results are a life characterized by the fruit of the Spirit.

Review Galatians 5:16-26

22. How have you experienced the freedom that comes from obeying the command to "walk by the Spirit"?

23. What does the presence of this fruit, or lack of, indicate about your reliance on the Holy Spirit?

24. How does remembering the promised results of "walking by the Spirit" encourage you today?

Lesson Twenty
Encouragement and Restoration

When believers yield to the Spirit in their own personal lives, there is unity, fellowship, and mutual encouragement with others. However, problems arise when we yield to our flesh. In this section of Galatians, Paul is giving instruction as to how to handle such situations. We often call this the process of restoration. It includes confronting sin, encouraging and strengthening a believer, and enjoying fellowship again.

Day 1

Read Galatians 5:26-6:1

1. Read Galatians 6:1 and fill out the chart.

WHAT'S THE PROBLEM?	
WHAT'S THE COMMAND?	
WHO IS INVOLVED?	
WHAT IS THE WARNING?	
WHAT IS THE OUTCOME?	

2. If someone is "transgressing," what are they yielding to?

3. How do you know if someone is "spiritual"? (Review Galatians 5:16, 22-23, 26.)

4. Read Matthew 7:3-5. How does this truth help you understand the warning in Galatians 6:1?

5. Why is this process of examining ourselves important in the body of Christ?

6. What are some reasons this process might be hard to carry out?

7. Read Galatians 5:26 again. Why do these attitudes make this process in Matthew 7:3-5 necessary?

Digging Deeper

Read John 8:1-11. Contrast the scribes' reaction to the woman with Jesus' reaction to her. What attitudes were present? What do you learn about confronting sin in another's life?

Restore...

The word "restore" in verse 1 carries the idea of setting broken bone. The doctor casts a broken arm so that it will heal properly with the hopes that the person will experience full use of the arm in the future. So it is with the process of restoration in a believer's life.

Day 2

There is a difference between confronting sin and encouraging someone who is struggling in a particular area of their life, but the two also go together. We cannot stop with confronting sin. After we help a person see their sin, we then can help them find their way back to yielding to the Spirit. Let's see what that looks like.

> **Read Galatians 6:2-5**

8. How might you bear another's burden?

9. Is it easier for you to point out what is wrong in another's life or to help them through a struggle? Why?

10. In what ways have you been encouraged in this way by another believer?

11. How could you extend this support to someone in your life?

Day 3

Like other instructions found in Scripture, when we follow in obedience, there is blessing. The restoration process is not easy and usually is painful, but the results are wonderful.

> **Read Galatians 6:6**

Galatians 6:6

Often Galatians 6:6 is used as a reference to support the paying of pastors and ministers. This principle is taught in other places in Scripture. Looking at the overall context of the book of Galatians, it does not seem that the monetary support of pastors is the primary application. This verse is in a passage about restoring believers caught in sin and the process and results that can be expected.

12. What two groups of people are involved in the sharing that is described in this verse?

13. What is to be shared?

14. Why would the "teacher" need encouragement?

15. Where do these "good things" come from (review Galatians 5:16, 22-23)?

16. Make a list of practical ways you can share the "good things" produced by the Spirit of God with others.

Day 4

Read Galatians 6:6

The word "shared" in this verse has the idea of mutual give and take. The sharing of "good things" should flow back and forth between believers. We call this fellowship.

17. Why do you think fellowship is an important part of the restoration process?

18. How does a breakdown in this process affect true Christian fellowship?

19. How has fellowship with other believers encouraged you to stay on course in walking by the Spirit?

20. What are some practical ways you could extend fellowship to a sister in need of encouragement?

Day 5

God, in His goodness, has provided what we need at every turn. Through His Spirit, He has given us the power and ability to live in obedience. We call that walking by the Spirit. As believers, we do not have to give into the temptations of our flesh. And yet, He has also provided help and instruction for when we stumble.

Read Galatians 5:26-6:6

21. What impacts you most from this passage?

22. How have you been encouraged by the biblical process of restoration?

23. How does understanding the truth of the gospel encourage you to embrace this?

Lesson Twenty-One
Living in Freedom Today

Memory Verse

"But it may never be that I would boast, except in the cross of our Lord Jesus Christ, through which the world has been crucified to me, and I to the world. For neither is circumcision anything, nor uncircumcision, but a new creation. And those who will walk by this rule, peace and mercy be upon them, and upon the Israel of God."
Galatians 6:14-16

Through the end of his letter to the Galatians, Paul continues to plead with believers to live by the power of the Holy Spirit and not by man-made regulations. We will need this reminder today.

Day 1

Paul uses the familiar principle of reaping and sowing to further explain how to walk by the Spirit. Planting a garden is a great example of this principle. If we plant bean seeds, we expect beans to grow. If peas grew instead of beans, that would be an indication that we made a mistake along the way. We can apply this same principle to walking by the Spirit. We reap what we sow.

> **Read Galatians 6:7-10**

1. What does it mean to "sow to please the sinful nature"?

2. Can you think of any practical example?

3. How will choosing to invest in fleshly living affect your relationship to the Lord and others?

Digging Deeper

Look up other places in the Bible where the words "sow" and "reap" are used. What other insights can you find about the principles of sowing and reaping?

Verse 8 tells us that sowing to the Spirit will result in eternal life. Often when we think of eternal life, we think of enjoying our future home with our Lord Jesus Christ. In reality, eternal life starts at the moment of salvation.

Read John 17:3

4. How does this verse describe eternal life?

5. How does walking by the Spirit allow us to enjoy all the blessings of being a child of God?

6. Why would yielding to the flesh change this experience?

Day 2

Read Galatians 6:2-5

7. What are some reasons people might grow weary in the battle between the flesh and the Spirit?

8. What does this indicate about their source of strength?

9. As you think about the ongoing battle between your flesh and the Spirit, in what circumstances are you tempted to become weary?

10. What encouragement do you see in verse 9?

11. How will your choice to say no to fleshly living in addition to saying yes to walking by the Spirit affect those around you?

Day 3

Read Galatians 6:11-18

Paul probably used a scribe to write this book and others. However, Paul ended most of his books by taking the pen and writing a closing statement in his own handwriting: "the grace of our Lord Jesus Christ be with you" (1 Thessalonians 5:28). In Galatians, he writes an entire closing paragraph. Based on your study of this book, why do you think he wrote so much more at the end of the letter to the Galatians?

12. Paul takes his last chance to again warn the Galatian churches about the Judaizers. What are some ways he describes the legalists, or Judaizers, in verses 12-13?

13. Why are people tempted to gravitate towards man-made rules to guide life instead of yielding to the Spirit?

14. When are you tempted to do this in your own life?

Day 4

Read Galatians 6:11-18

Paul's final words to the Galatians highlight his true heart. He knows that fleshly living will never lead to righteousness. The only hope for righteousness is the transforming work of the Spirit in the life of a believer. Rules and regulations will never save a person and will never lead to godly character.

15. In what does Paul boast?

16. What does that mean for you?

17. In verses 15-16, Paul again reminds the believers that circumcision doesn't matter. According to Paul, what does matter?

Read 2 Corinthians 5:17

18. What does it mean to be a new creation?

19. What happens to people when they live like they are "a new creation" according to Galatians 5:16?

20. How are you doing living like "a new creation?"

Day 5

Interestingly enough, Paul indulges the Galatians and refers to Spirit-led living as a "rule." We do need guidance and help to live a life that is pleasing to the Lord, but that guidance is not external. For believers, our guidance, power, and ability to live for the Lord comes from His Spirit.

Read Hebrews 8:6-13

21. What does it mean to have God's laws written on our hearts and minds?

22. How does this encourage you to give up your own rules for living and yield to the Spirit?

23. According to Galatians 6:16, what do believers who walk by the Spirit experience?

24. How have you experienced this in your life?

Paul's last words to the Galatians were words of encouragement. Even though they were struggling to accept God's grace, he reminded them that it is still available to them. We are like the Galatians. We are eager to accept God's grace for salvation but then turn around and think we must work to keep ourselves saved. We believe that hedging ourselves in with rules and boundaries will help us, but, in reality, all it does is place us under bondage. Remember Galatians 5:1? Christ set us free from bondage! God's grace is enough for salvation and enough to keep us growing and acting like we belong to Him.

Notes

21-5

25. Are you enjoying the freedom that a relationship with Christ provides?

26. What evidence is there in your life that supports your answers?

27. What can you do to avoid placing yourself back under the bondage of sin?

28. How can you continue to grow in enjoying the freedom that comes from a relationship with Christ?

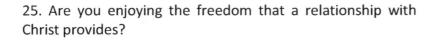

Notes

Lesson Twenty-Two
Conclusion

"Not that I have already obtained it or have already become perfect, but I press on so that I may lay hold of that for which also I was laid hold of by Christ Jesus. Brethren, I do not regard myself as having laid hold of it yet; but one thing I do: forgetting what lies behind and reaching forward to what lies ahead, I press on toward the goal for the prize of the upward call of God in Christ Jesus."
Philippians 3:12-14

Paul made his message clear in the book of Galatians: righteousness is obtained through faith in Christ alone. When we live this truth out in our lives, we live in freedom. He explained that the Law served a particular purpose, that we are children of God adopted through faith, and that we are to now walk by the Spirit as believers.

Galatians 5:1 states, "It was for freedom that Christ set us free; therefore keep standing firm and do not be subject again to a yoke of slavery" (NASB). Now that we know that we don't earn our righteousness through our actions, we can move forward in our lives in freedom and walk according to the Spirit. The fruit of the Spirit is love, joy, peace, patience, kindness, goodness, faithfulness, gentleness, and self-control. These qualities are to be increasingly present in our lives through the Holy Spirit's power, not our own. We can rest in His good work because "He who began a good work in you will perfect it until the day of Christ Jesus" Philippians 1:6b (NASB).

As we review what we have studied, let's give God the glory for what He has done and has revealed to us!

Day 1

Read Galatians 1-2

1. In Galatians 1:11-12, Paul states that the gospel he preached was from Jesus Christ. Write down the gospel in your own words.

2. Galatians 2:20 explains that as believers we now live by faith in Christ. Give an example of living by faith either from your life or from the life of someone you know.

3. How can you choose today to live by faith in Christ?

Day 2

Read Galatians 3

4. Galatians 3:9 refers to believers being blessed "with Abraham." What blessings do believers enjoy?

5. Who can you tell today about your faith and the blessings you enjoy from it?

6. Write a prayer of thanksgiving for those blessings.

Day 3

Read Galatians 4

7. Are you living more like the bondwoman, Hagar, which represents the Law, or like the free woman, Sarah, who represents faith in Christ?

8. What do you need to change today to live free?

9. Which verse in chapter 4 is the most meaningful to you?

Day 4

Read Galatians 5-6

10. List as many fruits of the Spirit from memory as possible.

11. Who do you know that demonstrates these fruits in their daily life?

12. How are these increasing in your life?

Day 5

Read Psalm 136

13. What main lesson did God teach you through Galatians this year?

14. How are you going to live differently because of this lesson?

Notes

15. Write a psalm of thanksgiving to God thanking Him for what He has done in your life?

Praise God for all He has taught us and how He has changed us! Let us live in the truth that we are free in Christ and rejoice in the Holy Spirit's transforming work in our lives.

Made in the USA
Coppell, TX
12 January 2022